RCTIC OCEAN

EUROPE

ASIA

AFRICA

PACIFIC OCEAN

INDIAN OCEAN

A Walk in the Rainforest

Written and Illustrated by
Kristin Joy Pratt

DEDICATION

To the forest—may it always be with us—
and to the children who are learning to love it.

ISBN paperback 1-878265-53-9
hardcover 1-878265-99-7

Published by DAWN Publications
14618 Tyler Foote Road
Nevada City, CA 95959
(916) 292-3482

Printed on recycled paper
using soy based ink

10 9 8 7 6 5 4 3
First Edition

Designed by LeeAnn Brook
Type style is Berkeley

INTRODUCTION

Rainforests circle our planet for twenty degrees of latitude on either side of the equator. They are like a beautiful green belt worn by Mother Earth. Each of the millions of animals and plants that makes its home in these jungles is like a jewel, making the belt all the more valuable.

The variety of plants and wildlife contained within the rainforests is amazing! More than half of all the species of plants and animals in the world make their home there. Some are found only in the rainforests and can live nowhere else. As many as two hundred different kinds of trees may grow in one acre. One tree may be home to more than fifty ant species and ten thousand other kinds of insects, spiders, and mites. Scientists call this variety "biodiversity."

Each of these animals and plants needs others to help it survive. For instance, worms, frogs, flies, earwigs, scorpions, spiders, and many others all live in one bromeliad plant. This mutual need is called "interdependence."

Sadly, half of the world's rainforests are already destroyed. At the current rate of destruction, another fourth will be lost by the year 2000. Around the world, one hundred acres of rainforest are cleared every minute! When this happens, the trees are taken away for lumber, some people try to raise cattle, and others sow crops which struggle to grow in the poor soil. Once the rainforest is cut down, the web of interdependence is broken. Thousands of species are condemned to extinction. The rains, without the forest, erode the bare soil.

To preserve the many fascinating plants and animals of the rainforest we must protect their environment. It is our job to save what is left of the jeweled rainforest belt because it is a valuable and necessary part of our beautiful planet. And as we work to protect and preserve the rainforest, we in turn promote the survival of all living species on earth.

"Hurt not the earth, neither the sea nor the trees."
—Revelation 7:3

XYZ, the ant,
went for a walk in the
rainforest, and what do
you think he saw?

He saw an amazing **Anteater** with a long
tongue carrying her baby on her back,

Anteaters are normally nomadic. They roam the
jungles of Central and South America in search of
ants and termites. It would be difficult for anteaters
to eat much of anything else because they are
completely toothless. Anteaters use their sharp,
powerful claws to rip into termite nests and ant
burrows. Then they use their long, sticky tongues to
lick up the insects they find. Most anteaters live up
in the trees. Only the giant anteater lives on the
forest floor. He must walk on the knuckles of his
front feet to keep his claws from being dulled.

Bromeliads grow on trees and on the forest floor. Every time it rains, tiny puddles collect inside the plant's radiant red center. When the temperature in the rainforest gets very warm, the center of the plant closes to save the precious water. Some frogs have discovered that these puddles are quite safe places to raise their young! Fortunately for the frogs, more than two thousand different kinds of bromeliads thrive in Central and South America.

a beautiful **Bromeliad** with a bright red center,

a comely **Cock-of-the-Rock**
with a golden crown,

The pigeon-sized cock-of-the-rock is found only in northern sections of the South American rainforests. Although unrelated to the chicken, he is called a cock because of the male's rooster-like appearance. The "rock" part of the name was contributed by the female. She only nests on large boulders within undisturbed rainforest. Because of such odd nesting habits, these bright birds are very rare.

a dazzling **Dragonfly** resting on an orchid,

Dragonflies, with a wingspan of up to seven inches, are among the largest insects living on earth. From their earliest stages, they are predators. Dragonflies eat fish larvae and all sorts of bugs, including mosquitoes. Their excellent vision helps them most when hunting. Dragonflies can detect movement up to forty feet away. We don't know of any insects that have become extinct because of man. However, destruction of the dragonfly's habitat by man's pollution, drainage, and filling in of ponds is a serious threat to these striking insects.

The emerald tree boa is found only in South America. He is ideally suited for his forest environment. While waiting in the branches for his next meal, he looks like a long, slender vine. This camouflaged canopy hunter is primarily a predator of tree frogs, but he will sometimes try to sneak up on and devour an iguana. Like a monkey's tail, the prehensile tail of the boa acts as a hand. With the help of his handy tail, the emerald tree boa coils around branches when resting.

an elegant **Emerald Tree Boa** slithering down a branch,

Ferns are found in every rainforest. There are over seven hundred different species of ferns. The Malaysian tree fern is one of the tallest. It can grow to be fifty feet tall. Most ferns grow on the forest floor, but some are epiphytes, that grow on other trees for support. Many kinds of ferns are plentiful, and all like the warm, humid environment of the rainforest.

a feathery **Fern** on the forest floor,

a gentle giant **Gorilla** grinning in the green growth,

Gorillas are big, hairy, and very strong. An adult male gorilla can grow to be six feet tall and may weigh 450 pounds. He could easily win a tug of war with six men. Even though they may look quite fierce, gorillas are really gentle. They live peacefully on the ground of the African rainforest in family groups called troops. A troop of gorillas may have five to thirty individuals. The head of each troop is an adult male called a silverback. Gorillas need to live in dense forests where they can find the huge amounts of leaves, stems, and fruits they need to survive. Adult gorillas eat about forty pounds of food each day! If they get enough food, and if they are not killed by hunters, gorillas can live to be fifty years old.

a hurried **Hummingbird** sipping nectar from a passion flower,

Over three hundred species of hummingbirds make their home in the Americas. However, they are most common in the rainforests of South America. They range from 2 inches to 8 1/2 inches long and come in a variety of brilliant colors. Hummingbird feathers shimmer and shine so beautifully that they seem to change colors. That is why many of them are named after jewels like rubies, sapphires, and emeralds. These tiny jewels fly amazingly fast—up to seventy-one miles per hour. Hummingbirds use their long beaks and tongues to sip nectar from flowers. The flowers of the rainforests need these speedy nectar sippers to pollinate them.

The iguana is a large lizard. The green iguana, the only type that lives in the rainforests, grows up to six feet long! Besides being completely camouflaged, green iguanas are extremely agile and fast. They like to sleep in trees that overhang water. Iguanas can drop forty to fifty feet from a tree to the ground, and also will jump into water and swim away from predators. Their diet is generally made up of plant food, but they liven it up with an occasional insect or two. Unfortunately, iguanas are threatened by too much hunting. However, captive breeding projects have been started in Panama and Costa Rica to save the iguana.

an intriguing Iguana basking on a branch,

The jaguar is an enormous cat that may weigh well over two hundred pounds. It is at the top of the food web in American rainforests: It can kill and eat anything it finds, but nothing eats it. The jaguar finds anything from deer to alligators quite delicious. It hunts in the water and in the trees to find its favorite delicacies. Some jaguars are protected in safe reserves by a car manufacturer that is called Jaguar.

a jumbo **Jaguar** just about
ready to jump,

a kingly **Kapok** tree that is home
to many plants and animals,

The kapok tree is found in African and American
rainforests. Because this tree can grow to be
150–200 feet tall, giant buttress roots are necessary
to hold it up. While other trees flower in the dry
season, kapok trees flower only in the flood season.
The flowers produce cotton-like seeds which are
blown in the wind and eventually carried away by
the river. Natives attach kapok fuzz to the rear of
their blowgun darts. Kapok is also used as the
stuffing in some life jackets.

a legion of **Leaf-Cutter Ants** marching along a liana,

Leaf-cutter ants are fantastic fungus farmers. First the leaf-cutter ants cut up the leaves with their scissor-like mandibles (or teeth). Next they carry the pieces back to their underground nest and chew them into pulp. After that they wait for the fungus to grow on the leaves and then they eat the fungus. This process can be compared to the way we grow mushrooms. The rainforest probably has more ants than any other kind of animal. One leaf-cutter ant colony can have over five million ants in it!

Macaws are the largest of all parrots. The brightly colored military macaws are especially noisy. Macaws have long, pointed wings that enable them to fly swiftly. Their sharp, hooked bills are perfect for eating nuts, fruits, and seeds. Macaws have feet with a very strong grip. Two of their toes point forward and two point backward. They can use their foot to grasp food and bring it to their mouth. Macaws can be found in Central and South America. However, along with other rare kinds of macaws, the military macaw must retreat into shrinking pockets of undisturbed rainforest to escape capture by humans.

two majestic **Military Macaws**
sitting quietly for a change,

Native peoples have lived along the Amazon for over 12,500 years. African tribes have also existed in the rainforest for thousands of generations. The earliest natives were hunter-gatherers, but later some discovered farming and began to farm small plots of land. Because of their long history of living close to nature, natives are able to identify thousands of different plants and animals that even expert biologists find difficult to tell apart. They also recognize hazardous plants and animals, and they are expert hunters. Most native peoples travel in small family groups of twenty to one hundred. Natives live in harmony with their environment and depend on it for all of their needs.

a natural **Native** who needs the rainforest to survive,

an observant **Ocelot** listening to the night noises of the jungle,

The ocelot lives mostly in the understory of the South American rainforests. He is an expert climber, feeding on small birds, lizards, and mice. The pattern on his fur provides perfect camouflage in the dappled light of the understory. The ocelot's fur also makes beautiful coats for humans. Sadly, the ocelot is now very rare because he has been hunted too much for his lovely coat.

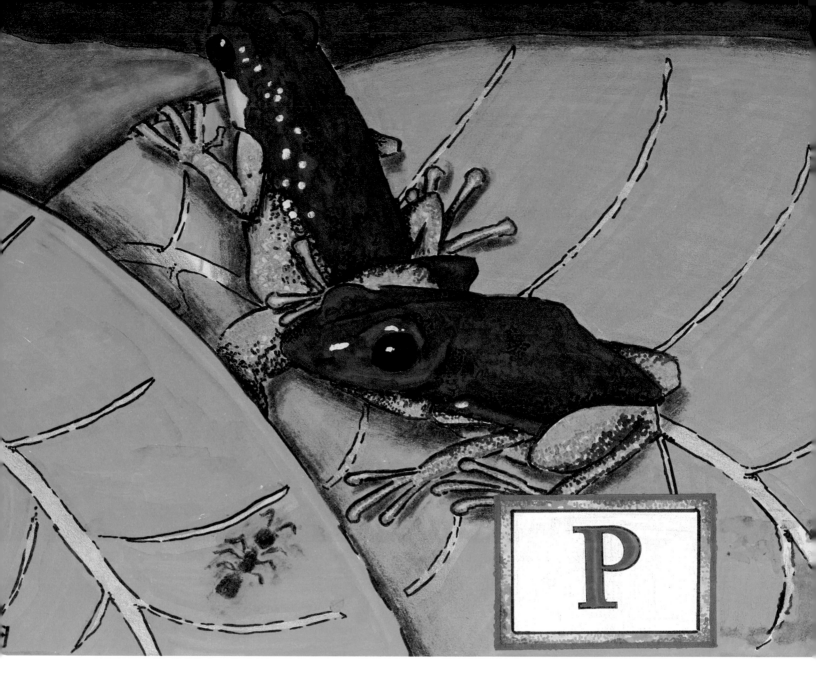

petite **Poison-Arrow Frogs** on a palm leaf,

The poison-arrow frog is very small and poisonous. Native hunters dip the points of their blowgun darts in the strong poison produced by this frog. No bigger than a man's thumbnail, the poison-arrow frog is found in South American rainforests. These tiny frogs lay their eggs on leaves. When the tadpole hatches, it is carried on the parents' back to a bromeliad where it grows to be a frog.

The resplendent quetzal of Central America is truly amazing. Natives have used its three-foot-long emerald tail feathers for elaborate head dresses worn by tribal chiefs. The quetzal eats forty-three different species of fruit. It has adapted enormous chest muscles that enable it to hover in front of these different plants while eating their fruit. The wild avocado is a favorite food of the colorful quetzal. There are so few of these birds left in the rainforest that they are considered an endangered species.

a quiet Resplendent **Quetzal** with long, lovely tail feathers,

The inch-long red-eyed tree frog makes his home in the disappearing tropical rainforests of eastern Central America. His name comes from his bulging red eyes that help him see better in dim light. His brightly colored skin serves as a warning to predators that he might be poisonous. While many tree frogs cling to branches and leaves with suction-tipped toes, the red-eyed tree frog can also grip twigs as monkeys do.

a ravishing **Red-eyed Tree Frog**
with big, bulgy eyes,

a slow **Sloth** suspended in a tree,

Sloths are fantastically slow-moving creatures found only in the rainforest canopies of South America. There are two kinds of sloths: those with three toes and those with only two. Sloths look grey-green in color because they move so slowly that tiny camouflaging algae grow all over their coats. Their enormous hooked claws and long arms make it possible for them to spend most of their time hanging from trees. The upside-down position of the sloth makes it convenient to feast on drooping leaves and fruits. The sloth does everything upside down. He even sleeps that way.

a terrific **Toucan** with a colorful beak,

The keel-billed toucan of South and Central America seems to be mostly beak! He uses his big bill to squash the many kinds of fruit he eats. Figs are his favorite snack. The bright colors of the bill of the toucan help to attract a mate. When he is sleeping, the toucan lays his big beak on his back and covers it with his wings and tail. The toucan is very important to the rainforest because he helps to distribute seeds from the fruits he eats.

Although butterflies are found almost everywhere, tropical rainforests have more kinds of butterflies than any other part of the world. In the rainforests of South America and Central America there are over ten thousand species! Butterflies are abundant in the rainforest because the warm, damp climate is the perfect place for flowering plants to grow, and flowers always attract butterflies. The beautifully colored butterflies feed on the nectar and help to pollinate the flowers they eat from at the same time. The urania butterfly is one lovely example of the many intricate patterns that butterflies have on their wings. The bright colors may help the butterfly to attract a mate, and they also may be a form of camouflage that helps him vanish into the forest backgrounds.

an unusual **Urania Butterfly** with an undulating pattern,

Orchids are found all over the rainforest world. There are as many as one thousand different kinds of orchids in Costa Rica alone. Besides growing on the ground, many orchids live in trees. Like the bromeliad and some ferns, orchids use the trees they live in to be closer to light, but gain their food from rainwater and debris that washes down the bark. These kinds of plants are called epiphytes. One of the most interesting orchids is the vanilla orchid, the only type that is a vine. From the fruit of this extraordinary plant the world obtains vanilla. It is the flavor used to make vanilla ice cream and other good things to eat.

a vibrant **Vanilla Orchid** with very flavorful fruit,

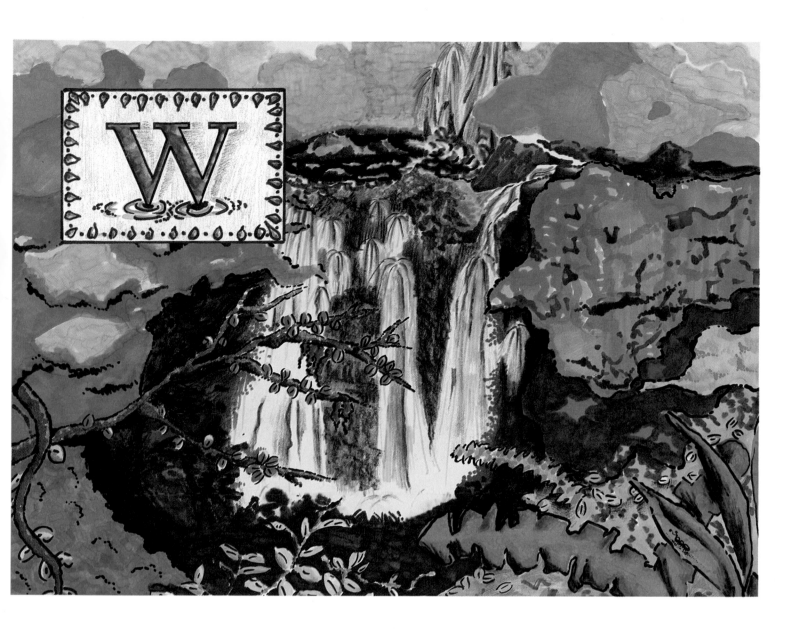

and wonderfully wet **Water** washing over the rocks!

Water is everywhere in the rainforest. Rivers and streams criss-cross like highways on a road map. There is so much water in the air that it feels the same as when you've just come out of a steamy hot shower. It rains one hundred to four hundred inches every year there, and that is why we call it a rainforest. In the rainy season, some of the rivers and lakes flood all the way to the tree tops. Each of the animals in all of the rainforests needs water to survive. Frogs live in it, jaguars hunt in it, anteaters drink it, and native peoples swim in it. The rainforest could not live without water.

XYZ, it's plain to see, the rainforest is full of **biodiversity.**

ABOUT THE AUTHOR

Kristin Joy Pratt lives with her family near St. Louis, Missouri. During her freshman year at The Principia Upper School, she chose to write and illustrate a children's book to fulfill a requirement for an independent-study project. Based on a study of global deforestation and associated environmental issues, she was inspired to use the rainforest as the theme for her project. Like many of her teachers and fellow students, Kristin feels concern for the present state of the environment and sees the need for people to work together for constructive solutions.

Kristin became interested in art and literature at an early age. By the time she was eight, she was enrolled in after-school art lessons. She completed the illustrations for *A Walk in the Rainforest* when she was fifteen.

Kristin plans to continue her education, seeking other ways to support environmental issues through her love of art.

ACKNOWLEDGEMENTS

I am especially grateful to the following friends who encouraged and supported me while I worked on this book: Rachel Crandell, Laura Fisher, Marcia Martin, Judith Morse, Ted Munnecke, Kim Overton, Kathy Pratt, Katie Pratt, Ken Pratt, Kevin Pratt, Bob Rieder, Jane Reider, Jackie Ritchie, and Peter Shields.

Special thanks to the Missouri Botanical Gardens for providing the authentic rainforest environment for the author's photograph.

— Kristin Joy Pratt